Written into the Curve of the Sea's Open Throat

Written into the Curve of the Sea's Open Throat

Laurel Benjamin

SHANTI ARTS PUBLISHING

BRUNSWICK, MAINE

Gratitude to so many.

To my Ekphrastic Writers.

To Shelly Cato, Sandra Fees, Michelle Holland, for helping me grow the book, re-examine point of view and voice, and offer support in ways I couldn't have predicted.

To Susan Michelle Coronel, thank you for a collaboration which allowed some of the key pieces to birth.

To Ellen Weinreb, who gathers the Weinreb family together and for bringing the family letters into our lives.

To Lynne Kemen, my writing partner. Thank you for your humor, wit, and enthusiasm.

To Dan Dickinson for your love, companionship, and support which made this book possible.

To my grandparents, great grandparents, those who survived, and those who did not. You are here, breathing between the fog and the sea.

For my dear mother, who made the family tree, and who is still my guide, my inspiration.

Contents

Ask the Goats

How to Quilt Absolution

The Art of Persuasion

Acknowledgements

Many thanks to the editors and staff of the following journals in which some of the poems in this book appeared, often in earlier forms:

As It Ought To Be Magazine: "Motel Room without a Night Light" (nominated for Best of the Net)

The Broken Spine: "The Red Stairway"

Calul Journal: "On Easter I Quote Ecclesiastes to My Husband"

Cider Press Review: "A cat's paw has its own geography,"

The Deronda Review: "Ode for Walking Women" and "Woman Under the Bridge"

Eclectica Magazine: "Anti-Love Poem"

The Ekphrastic Review: "I grow extra ovaries" and "Savage" (contest finalist)

Eunoia Review: "Diptych After Silent Spring"; "Half-Disappeared"; and "I follow my mother through the gallery,"

fillingStation: "Hourglass"

Gone Lawn: "The Starling"

Gyroscope Reiview: "Felting"

The Haibun Journal: "Invisible Border"

Halfway Down the Stairs: "Cat as Muse"

Heavy Feather Review: "Oranges"

Mocking Heart Review: "Twilight Summer"

Moon City Review: "I See Your Ovary, She Said"

Nixes Mate: "When My Husband on our wedding anniversary"

Of the Book: "The Art of Persuasion"; "A Blind Day Where Our Porch Is Soaked"; "The Ghost of My Grandmother, with Clouds"; "In the Middle"; "Letter to the Angels, Poland, 1919"; "My Soul Blossom in Your Blood"; "People Speak Yiddish in Bars All Over Berlin"; "Pigment into a Wound"; and "Shlufulah"

The Poet's Corner: "Fable" (Ekphrastic Challenge contest winner)

Quartet: "Beyond the Grave" (nominated for a Pushcart Prize)

Rise Up Review: "A Woman Observes"

Rogue Agent: "The Forceps of War"

Sheila-Na-Gig: "At the Market after Reading about the Alien Meteorite" and "Nine Months Post-October 7"

Spillwords: "Ars Poetica as Crochet"

Stone Poetry Quarterly: "Self-Portrait as a Tea Shop"

Taos Journal of Poetry: "Half the green donkey left Russia,"

Variant Lit: "Woman Posing as Bell Pepper"

Voices Israel: "Woman as an Aramaic Incantation Bowl" (Honorable Mention for the Ruben Rose Memorial Poetry Competition)

Wordpeace: "Bedtime Stories"

A voice from the dark called out,
"The poets must give us
   imagination of peace, to oust the intense, familiar
   imagination of disaster.
Peace, not only the absence of war."

—Denise Levertov

A Woman Observes

i.

Today I'm making fennel golden-raisin scones,
eggs with shiitakes and swiss, a good stiff black tea.

Yet I can't help picture the homeless woman
who strips from the waist down

on the pavement outside the autobody shop,
sunburnt in winter.

I pass by weekly.
Maybe if I stared longer

she would stand, cover herself.
I don't call anyone.

ii.

Coreopsis line the day, faces of bright gold petals
with orange centers. Yet we have no use for them,

have mastered a stance like crows waiting for cows
to shit so we can pick through

as flies hover. We chant
separately or in groups.

Knees, leggy legs, thighs, fallow
stems ready to innuendo a feast.

We inverse ourselves if necessary.
Preside on the Supreme Court, cull

the larynx for the right tone, weigh decisions.
Master the stars written out of a scientist's paper.

I'm rash with coercive thoughts.
Want to cover the naked woman because

she can't. Would like to be chlorophyll, responsible
for the color green.

Would like to reverse the universe.

Half-Disappeared

The Starling

Before the day is over, workmen next door
will pour cement. What they don't see on dark soil
wet from the weekend's storm—
a starling. Statue shoulders, feather-shine swept down
as microscope eyes search for earthworms.

Little is left of the sun, snipped by approaching
rain clouds. No bartering between sun and clouds
or between workmen and bird. Her shiny
black outfit embedded with jewels an opera-goer
would wear, humming *Così Fan Tutte*.

I pull up the blinds to see how work is progressing,
hear a piercing song. New addition
to their house over a carcass. Can we call it
a crime to kill an invasive species—
or is it an errand of mercy?

Years ago, I brushed on green eyeshadow,
pulled a peacoat over sloping shoulders, arriving
for secretarial duty at the Berkeley Lab.

Witnessed my boss in the nuclear department thrust
gloved hands into portals of a secure case
as he handled a reactive substance. I felt pin pricks
on my head as if I was the experiment. As if
he'd pushed a starling
in my mouth.

                  Then I became the starling,
feathers forced through skin.
Beak tearing gums, song without orchestra.
Only harsh piccolo trill.
Fast fingers inside lungs.

What about my housemate with his No Nukes poster
and what did I sign up for, how far
curiosity could lead in the name of science,
acceleration of uranium and other particles.

That day I went into the ladies room, peeled off
tan stockings, raised my hand
to the powdered soap dispenser, tried
to rub off eyeshadow, eyes stinging,
handed in my badge at building 90.
Shuttled downtown.

Today, the workmen next door have finished.
Did the starling witness her own burial? No evidence
would convict the bird killers. They lean
on one leg, laugh and smoke,
pack up their tools, then drive away.

A cat's paw has its own geography,

durable and quick like the solar system, pads like planets
rotating, leathered over years, slow tender

fruits beyond the membrane, everything pink like the first night
spent with a lover. Slow, durable, train of youth

singing a chorus of Mahler, where he makes the turn by scoring
brass instruments. A country where no one has burned forests or blazed

trails, no one has divided what we call wilderness.
The cat sleeps with one ear open, radar hairs like a theater curtain

blown gently, her attention at all times in target-line
with a possible earthquake. Her eyes water.

Maybe she's found a voice to desiccate
what's not needed for survival.

Ode for Walking Women

On a day when I am walking with two women
        in my neighborhood, over past the bakery
where they sell fruit pies, cream pies, quiche,
        and pizza, and the European woman

tells us she's taking antibiotics for Lyme's
        disease, asks questions about my ear pain.
The subject changes to the news
        and how we find our sources. I don't

mention the ten Jewish newspapers
        in my inbox every morning, don't say
as we cross Ashbury Avenue and start
        climbing uphill, about the Nova exhibit

in New York extended another two weeks
        and how a woman found her shoes
in a pile of shoes on a table where the shoes
        belonged to the three hundred sixty

dead on October 7, each pair with a barcode,
        so she picked up her shoes and walked
out of the exhibit. Collapsed outside. I'm not
        climbing uphill anymore. Have led

the two women to a park where we find
        a deer with two spotted babies,
then wild turkeys, and chestnut-backed
        chickadees who chatter. I answer

a question. Say, *The protestors called
        for the end of Israel and death to Jews.*
And then we're walking on pavement
        when the British woman asks about

the *Times* and I point out they shy away,
        and she says, *They're afraid.* I wait
a couple minutes to hear both women.
        Sigh because this is the first time

since a massacre in another country I've never
        visited, never wanted to, until recently
never felt part of, the first time since I
        confined myself to a tiny space where

at night cargo trains lean on the horn, pushing
        through to the next town. The first time
someone ascends, not Jewish, but understands.
        And I imagine in vespers the women repeat

a devotion resembling the native garden
        we've stopped to admire, how even
a single cactus blends in, not friendly
        nor hostile to manzanita which will

outlast us all, and flannelbush with buttery
        petals, all five of them. I have no defense
for what's come after October 7,
        don't believe in an eye for an eye, but as we

make our way downhill with sweeping
        views of the Golden Gate, I'm out of
breath finally. We stop to take it in before
        descending back into indifferent streets.

Half-Disappeared

warm under the canopy of war // she hears
the onslaught of butterflies //

have they left // men's voices
broken // windows

// last season's olives
thrown // from baskets

// demands have been made for
violets who say // *where have you been* //

no answer // captor
sheathed // to say

> *you will remain after others leave*
> *have my baby // marry me //*

❊

will she write // in the margins of
her sheaf // will she plump

her own daughter //
there are no clowns // even

the laughter // dips and loops
// all the ghosts // enter

from one door // her eager mind
drawn // a charcoal flame

she writes // *oh quench my thirst //*
shadow my camera of belief

Half the green donkey left Russia,

my young grandfather raising an ax, then down
on the dorsal spine. He wobbled the two-legged half-
animal deep into birches, where it would undergo survey
from wolves and vultures. His mother stuffed lunch
in his pack. Gestured, *Remember us*, with muddied gloves.
Cheeks the red of her apron.

I've read stories. In one, a woman dies in childbirth
and is given a donkey's burial. In another, a man arrives
in New York, meets a woman at a cafeteria, and one night
on his way home sees a ghost—could he have produced
the hide of a donkey out of passion, like a wedding dance
where feet braid together? Could my grandfather
have done the same thing, wallpapering homes—produced
a donkey between sheets floral and striped?

In his Flatbush apartment on Shabbat, pinstripe-suited,
my grandfather read the paper, peekaboo'd under each word
his mother's voice—*Keep yourself good*. Stuffing his pipe,
he remembered her mumbling to a neighbor—
The rest of my days, imagined her rearranging the clothesline
so the word *days* would come first, then the word *rest*
would appear in a field of bluebells.

All these years later, I can't help wondering if his letters
to his mother were enough to break her quiet nightmares.
I know so little about him. He was in his 80s
when my brother and I were young, ushered us along
a busy boulevard to a store where he bought us Silly Putty.
His face wrought deep lines, body shrunken, as if
back in Russia he'd stored everything
into small compartments.

I never asked. Did his mother find the half-donkey
among trees and buttercups? Would it vanquish
the cave of tears forested into her as she hugged its side?
What can I do with half, she must have said. Maybe
forget the chaos of being a Jew in Russia?

Invisible Boundary

I take the trail where the sign leads, head into pain then
medicate, take it past birches to low-lying manzanita, zigzag
into wild garlic, where a darkling thrush whistles, eyes sparkling.
I wake. Slouched on the living room chair. I don't possess
Elizabeth Barrett Browning's laudanum, must contact the
plumber, have the furnace serviced, research window cranks,
but don't reside in Casa Guidi so can't search churches for
frescoes, can't find a wine bar with pinot grigio and a soft cheese
accompanied by fig jam. I'm not asking the Buddha to reawaken
this day, but could use some advice on enlightenment.

> where this trail diverts
> oh snow-capped mountains
> oh trembling lilies!

You Will All Be Mortal

Twilight Summer

Choose this fern, circle-carved from soil,
hold it up to stars poking their fangs,
cut through the veil with your fisted hands.
Understudy your daughter if you have one,

hold her up to stars poking their heads,
background orbs filling uncut chances,
understudy your daughter if you've birthed one.
The longer you stand in the open a bargain is run,

background orbs filling uncut chances,
department store sky with wrinkled shirt upon shirt.
The longer you stare in the night a bargain is run,
women fumbling to find a child of cloth,

department store sky, wrinkled shirt upon shirt.
Escalator *chunk chunk* metal stairs up and down,
says, *In exile you will simmer then burn, take your leave.*
You hold the fern to the cold bedtime sky,

ask, *In exile will you simmer then burn, take your leave,*
cut through the veil with your open hands?
You hold the fern up to the cold bedtime sky.
You chose this fern, circle-carved from soil.

The Wholesale Flower Boy

We haven't spoken since the war.
Remember your family's cabin in the gold country,

where you stuffed wood in the stove,
how we spoke of your family, what they brought—

accordions, pasta, wool blankets in summer, crimson
roses. I flung sheets, unwrapped dust motes.

You said, *I was gentle the first time,*
leaving me to muffle insides, abraded.

On the drive back, you pressed the horn at the bridge,
and near the jetty where sails ran green

and gulls covered the harbor mouth, you took
your foot off the brake.

After you, I leashed myself to another
whose basement bed shook.

Now the new war continues
and we still haven't spoken.

I don't carry missiles anymore,
endure no country except this one,

don't fault the lesson
you thought necessary.

Bedtime Stories

The word *pussy*, a character from slumberland,
where innocence turns to slang turns to cuss,
making short skirt and fishnets a double S—
the hiss a snaky distaste that bends boy's knees

at the edge of vulgar, vulva, vagina.
They prefer to knock us up and tear us down
at the edge of vulgar, vulva, vagina, the Y
after *puss* as if we belong to them,

preferring to knock us up and deliver the birth,
our tresses no less tough, our messes a bridge.
The Y after *puss*—no we'll never belong to them—
dismiss pussy-whipping, dismiss the hushing.

We're no less tough, our secrets a bridge—
the hiss a snaky taste that bends men's knees,
never pussy-whipping, never hushed in groups—
leave the word *pussy*, a character from slumberland.

Woman Posing as Bell Pepper

This is the part where I remove my skirt, shirt, and everything else.
Curl hands over shoulders, squinch knees until shoulders

collapse, until buttocks separate a little, backbone reaching
and over, my head invisible. I say, *That's how you want me, right?*

Wound into nothing, wrinkles, and if you look closely, almost
fungus, mold, signs of cell vegetable growth. And there's you,

my love, and the easel, sticky smell of oil, your lips pursed
as you whistle between strokes, *I'm just gonna add some shine.*

But I'm not here anymore, think of one hike we took, skinny
trail running up a series of small falls called cataracts,

passing ferns and bigleaf maple, oak and huckleberry, and a couple
yelling at each other words we couldn't understand except one—

Fuck, her eyes bulging. Now I'm alert, back under your paintbrush,
liquid pouring over me, hair clumping like dreadlocks. I separate

strands, then grab the ends and tuck them into
my mouth, sucking. This is a kind of forced meditation.

I give you no expression, no shine from light—
keeping still, letting go, a bend to the mirror of self.

What My Ovaries Don't Know

Mattress springs jiggle in a forest. Men knock, one after the
other. A line forms like tryouts for a musical. The old one's
wiry with a paid-up house, then the young one unreels an Irish
brogue and Guinness breath. Deciduous light. Circles breakfast
between metal strands. Bulbs spurt coarse hair from mud.
Newborn saplings inch out. Night dressed in a day cloak rifles
through magazines.

> crocheted children, I
> won't allow you to pass through
> hundreds of wool hats

Oranges

A woman has taken a man into the kitchen, shows him the pan
stripped of its black coat—*Taken years to form*, she says,

and grabs the unscented orange cleanser, like picking
off the tree, a globe ready to burst. She dreams the past,

gurney ride down a hallway, and under the gas she's breast-
stroking in the pool with her mother who wears an old style cap,

white with thick flower petals, and at the same time
she's standing above herself in the operating room monitoring

the anesthesia, yet she's also in a small boat crossing
a foggy river where an oarsman spoons into her mouth

the jelly she ate before a different surgery where Dr. Yang slit
her belly button, red liquid from a baby's crown

except she never got that far. Later in recovery, she thinks, *I was right,*
though all she can hear is her mother's opera, the tenor's Italian

garbled with old-record scratches, uttering, *Stripped
of your motherhood*, bouncing off the metal stand with tissue box

and lip balm, her glasses case, and the curtains arc pale
peach like a childhood room and the air freshener

in that galley kitchen, *Citrus Breeze*. She remembers
the vacation, the motel in Winemucca en route to Yellowstone

where they paid more than $6 but less than $12 and the family
style restaurant with huge plates of stew and how he rode

the fast highway like an ambulance driver yet reverent
of the speed limit, the long freight train dragging

cows to their death, and the boxcar they waited for
as she used her fingernails to peel a long singular piece

into her lap, then segmented and inserted each piece
into her mouth, the juice smarting a sore, but the train

never ended and the salt flats, they were blinding white.

Anti-Love Poem

Sometimes romance is like carpenter bees sucking

juice from hot lips sage, lumps of deep coal, crows plunging

then away as if a crime has been committed, shoals heard

near a night cabin, old boyfriend rushing over to rid the new one.

Hummingbird red, liposuction-hushed roses, watercolor-

streaked tiger lilies, throats rifle-ripe, threat-yellow

bleeding. Real romance is nothing, lasting weeks or a year, a swollen

conversation. Date for planting, date of fruition,

notes jotted to track growth—

these are not applicable to bumblebees, to crows' illegal

activities, not useful when fall days rule,

full of static electricity, leaves not yet ground to soil.

You Will All Be Mortal

When in trouble, call the house cat, who makes believe

string is a wild thing, who despairs when paper

wriggles then dies. She is my doctor. In her house, verbs slip

under sharp claws. Milk and transparency whine

like alphabets humans can't temper. She teases miracles

out of a promise to the cat god, remembers

when slaves built the pyramids, spit-sealed stones, drowned

in revelation. She's witnessed the first peaches grown

and the price, as little as 5 nefer-nubs.

Descending from the sky, she does not decree

immortality means having children.

I See Your Ovary, She Said

The chair screeched every time she adjusted. I breathed evenly
unless she said, *Hold*, picturing videos where techs trained to
insert the wand, how to push, pressure, release, how to find
what's buried deep. And she, a woman named France from Iran
who dyed her hair dark to overlay natural grey. The wand moved
to the left. Silence. My leg shifted on its own, rested against
her leg. On the ceiling some kind soul had pasted butterflies—
blue like Spode plates, midnight a child would paint in a first
watercolor.

        bodice tight, blue tatting
        Emily Dickinson gown
        lines running down the edges

        insect leg sonnets
        Queen Anne's lace doily
        two lorazepam

Everlasting

I don't mean eternity, but chrysanthemums gathered
this morning at the corner shop where I refuse

help from the clerk with a yellow-pink
hairdo, unlike traditional arrangements.

I can't breathe rubrum lilies' sweet foul odor,
work my way down the aisle of roses, their burkas

flushed, then gladiolas' wide faces waiting
for an answer. Years ago, I found an unschooled job,

arrived in red-shoes, white-rolled sox, like a garden
statue. Learned to form arrangements

for the temple down the street, inserting
mum stems into a foam form. Learned to highlight

their evershine. To speak quietly. Position
the everlasting on the proscenium, their curved

membranes chatting open-faced, where mourners would view
the casket. Now, I have another name for mums,

tumor inside my cat's right lung lobe. I know the spot
is not cerulean or lavender, instead the funereal

petals from those arrangements years ago. We always included
five white ray florets. *It hasn't grown,* writes the vet.

I call a vet tech friend. Call again. Scrutinize
the cat's eyes until we're both blinking. She tires, as if I'm cutting

a dress pattern into her, as if I can hold the mass
in my hand. Trace where to remove.

I cannot arrange these chrysanthemums.

Roundup of Children from the Ghetto

He saw the pinafores quietly sitting on a shelf
of 33 little girls led into the building,
powder of their innocence foaming the sky.
In the yard, eyelashes once brown and gold turned white

of 33 little girls led into the chamber,
one minute a sky full of pockets, the next
a yard, eyelashes once brown and gold turned white.
He remembered fireworks put on by the city,

one minute a sky full of pockets, the next,
crushed glass like his mother's vase, broken.
Remembered butterflies released into the sky,
wild costumes, how everyone would circle dance.

The sound of crushed glass like his mother's vase,
remembered, his mind broken by the camp.
Here, no wild costumes, no circle dance, no rabbi.
No, this would not happen here, butterflies let loose

remembering everyone before the camp,
powder of innocence foaming the sky,
No, this would not happen here, butterflies loosening,
pinafores quietly folded on a shelf.

GHOST WITH CLOUDS

Letter to the Angels, Poland, 1919

My beard is scraggly   clothes hang on my skeleton   but
        I speak not for myself

We were never asked to empty our homes
                                        instead we howled
                        sparrows scattering   lime trees lined up

                We left River Stryi's platinum surface
speaking foolishness   not heeding a rabbi's sermon

                The river would never empty itself   we   would never
empty   willingness measured out

                                Two children gone ahead
                        Mary, Harry, letters sent   no reply

        so I write postcards to you, dear Angels

Nothing to eat   no work   the Spanish flu   Tobe   lost

                                I implore you

                Now in Bolesławiec   we surrender
                                our autograph books
                        friends' signatures to remember us

                        we empty   viola notes
                                clang cookpots
                as we pack

I'm trying to understand   a self-emptying

                We direct conversation your way
complain of in-laws   small matters

Are you
    good angel   bad angel

Now in Tarnów, we head overland
then into the purple sea
    where a seven-headed sea serpent

    twist   turn   coil   we cannot control
    visions aboard ship   a man swallowed

    Your instructions for arrival in Amerika
arrange a new house   the same pattern   arrange the eyes

    arrange ourselves
    into tablecloth   lamp   settee

    chanting no longer hidden   we become Americans
    forgo strict observance   do not drape
    the head with a shawl

We still need you, good Angel

    A man fell into the ocean
    the serpent screaming,

    You cannot return

    photo washed
    with the red blood of plankton

Shlufulah

My mother overturned laws wearing shoes too tight,
and at night her—*Shlufalah*—unhinged

tremors ever so gently, from a past when she knew
nothing of sycophants in the openings

of the world, clay sculpture dreams
where—*Shlufalah*—her mother tucked

sheets to keep out the draft, shut out the mechanic
down the street twisting metal, like dust

settling on the north pole—*Shlufalah*—
the only way to anchor a babe, hand-molded

mountains, illumination of perfect
syllables—and my own—*Shlufalah*—sea shifting

bedrock, the sea whispering, my mother's lips
feather fluffed, for—*Shlufalah*—

swagger of sleep forming at the corners,
that I could inherit—*Shlufalah*—from my mother,

holding faith in her palm.

* means sleep or nap in Yiddish

Beyond the Grave

i.

The neurologist skooches over to display my brain
on the computer screen. I say   *My mother's brain*
a whole hemisphere missing   because surely
that would explain the nerve pain.

He squeezes something out of a tube, places his thumbs
behind my ears.
                         I say   *This will hurt after.*

          I only know a quarter of what he knows
about nerve endings but

                                        surrender.
Close my eyes

                    open them
                                        stare at the brain scan

an overlay that can't be explained—

my mother's scan, not shown to us after her stroke
but at the second hospital
                                        like a watercolor.
          Has someone applied   blush
                    on the right hemisphere?

ii.

My cousin calls me, says, *Your mother was happy
you didn't have children*, beyond the grave talk
I don't need because
                         what did my mother really mean?

          Did she tell my cousin this while squeezing
toothpaste out of a tube, washing dishes,

counting quarters for the pool locker
                    while on the phone?

My mother described to me her cat grandchildren
as definitive.

                              She was a warrior
          of driving down chance by planning
             so most things could be predicted
                   in the wide plaid pants she wore.

iii.

The brain doctor doesn't hear me   leans in
        as if I baked a cake   he wants to slice.

                    Yet
he doesn't notice my mother has   entered the room
or someone who looks like her   is leaving
a trail of ash
            over the exam room floor.

          He can't perceive
a cloak covering the shoulders of the woman, swimsuit
peeking out, her face
                    pasty with sunscreen
          a good ghost
        goggles around her neck.

          She is dripping wet over the tiled floor,

dripping wet over my body
while the doctor manipulates   the space behind
my ears, against my skull   infiltrating
            nerve endings.

iv.

I remember when I brought my mother to her regular doctor
after the stroke because she would stand up and
                                        fall down.

            He came into the room, took one look.
Changing her medication wouldn't fix her brain,
                                    half hemisphere

wiped out, brain playing a chess game
                                        where a hand brushed
the pieces off the table.

        v.

I hear my doctor say,
            Your brain shows you've lived a healthy life.

I separate myself from the memory
to hear him
                separate from   my mother's ghost
in the room, from   my mother's brain scan.

                                            My fingers rip out
                                            the stitches
                                            stitching us together.

Wasn't I the hand that swept
the chess pieces off the table?
                Wasn't it
                                            my fault
                not calling her back   the day of
                                            her stroke

tired of her not listening to the doctor?

I tell the neurologist
The space behind my ears is where I hide things.

I followed my mother through the gallery,

ran from a green and purple monster mid-flight,
past a river where women wrung out laundry.
Then into another painting.

We opened the watercolor mouth,
smack into a burnt tree.

Now I can't narrow vision without her.

We were never friends like some mother-
daughters, yet shared a green sweater from Marks & Spencer,
a reversible wrap-around dress.

It was the omissions.

Her voice delayed as she paused in front of a house,
a garden, a trail, to define myrtle or igneous rock.

Today, I maneuver a gallery of Mary Cassatt's women—
translucent flesh, breast feeding, plump and content.
In one, a mother's nipple almost shows.

These are not the scenes with fruit trees.

Tomorrow I'll write about the painting where a toddler's hand
squeezes a mother's chin.

For my mother, I hope some mornings
were a dream found,
when our finger pads touched.

I hold a magnifying glass over an old photo,
picnicking at the merry-go-round, discover
her skirt, stained with mulberries.

The Ghost of My Grandmother, with Clouds

i.

She visited my childhood room nightly. Sleeves
left a vapor trail and sometimes   in the guise of a deer
licked my hand, her tongue warm.
                                        Dust settled,
a dim moon translating Yiddish, the round parts   half sentences—
Death accidental—   (like my mother said)

ii.

Your grandmother? Your husband? The doctor said in few words. As if
cancer could be procured by association   or a paper gown.
                    My grandmother at 46 had no technology to vision
the growth—a deer's fur rubbed in the wrong direction, prey
                                        to the hunter.

                    I couldn't wait another year—
watched the video, signed the form, tied the floor-length cloth gown.
                    Woke in a daze (or thought I woke)
next to my husband   a walking dream   meeting a tortoiseshell cat
rough coat, milky eyes.   A woman popped out of an RV
                                saying, *She's lived all her lives.*

                    The woman's wrinkled hands took our hands.
I channel St. Francis. Sent us away with a postcard of angels.

iii.

What is waking? I woke up glowing. Should have run
when my husband   yes my husband   was diagnosed
with the same cancer as my grandmother
or what is it to promise   yourself to someone

                    based on tragedy   like soldiers
                            and the women who marry them.

        iv.

                        We made it past his surgery
to a three week trip of England   hiking around a lake
where a duck rippled.

                                        I ran
along the trail   ran away   towering peak behind
tagging trees   like my brother and I on long family hikes
        saying, *You're it.*

Lichen attached to my hands   I pictured the doctor who refused
                                        to take me seriously
                        as an already-ghost.

        Then tests revealed I had no cancer.

He couldn't see the ghost of my grandmother or hear
her voice
                tempered by time. If a woman left one town
for another to escape Jew-burning—
                        she ran—

        Wouldn't she advise
                and wouldn't you listen when she appeared
bedside, speaking beyond the grave?

        v.

(Now, I imagine grandmother's death   a kind of sacrifice,
        hard Flatbush streets an exchange
for relatives struck down in Poland, Ruthenia, Galicia   lines
        blurring.
                But I know it doesn't work that way.

She could not save her cousin, bullet
            to the head, pogrom in Styri   shot like others
                        who would not burn.)

        vi.

At some point (maybe age twelve) I asked my grandmother,
                        Don't come back.
                My bones barely fit on the cot-sized bed
                        flesh one incarnation
                    of who I'd become.

Her round face shook and her short dark hair
            formed a face with nose and twinkling eyes.

                        The velvet deer sleeves
            worn on special occasions
                    extended—

She offered   a ring.   Gold.

        It wouldn't fit—ghosts are broken
    shadow inside rain   inside breath.

FORCEPS OF WAR

Diptych after Silent Spring

i.

For my students reading Rachel Carson, nothing new.
Like fish dying of pesticides, young people fall on Oakland streets
as cars whiz by, not the blow of backfire but young men hopped up

on drugs. Staccato voices outside a church, one student who cooed
like a dove, her sister said, before curving her wings.
I can handle this, search the textbook

for bird kills—no, maybe the story of the earth—when the most poetic
student who wears a beret and pins a flower in his lapel, who loves
telling fables, speaks of vindication and the day

all nature will rebel, lifts his hands from the desk, unfurls
his fingers and removes the flower.

ii.

My husband and I pull over at the old Chinese fishing village,
now a tourist spot with antique shops, a row of buildings,
tall reeds along the shore. Someone has pasted orange dots

on telephone poles to guide visitors. A plaque at the Mercantile
says, *Once a parlor of sin,* but a brochure mentions nothing,
like the boardwalk, emptying our footsteps.

Is it important to preserve life
for an outsider's lunch spot along an old highway
called The River Route, running to Sacramento?

Crows ragtag over the same meal seagulls will ensure is theirs.

A Blind Day Where Our Porch Is Soaked

Yet it's so much more,
crimson trees half lit,

and behind, more trunks, thinner
as if they have drunk too much

or not enough, trying all the bars in town
on a bender. Rain tumbles

over gutters
and I think of the war,

what's just and unjust.
Sweet sparrow song—

an idealist perhaps—
pierces through, as if she can stop

the bombs or body
count or reverse time

so young women tied
to trees in an orchard

were not, after all,
mutilated.

Maybe the flooding here—
how water pools,

surging the door jam,
maybe this abundance

accounts for what's been taken.

Diaspora

I outgrew a taciturn barn where lambs weaned,
wandered through a main street market

overflowing. I shot a camera roll's worth of
shepherd's purse, tiny triangular leaves

pushing a perimeter fence. I smoldered
a multiple-exposure portrait, bird's beak

piercing a flowermoon. I built a synagogue
with a Byzantine dome, burned by Nazis before

the allies could bomb. I swept prayers into a dark corner
where a woman's shawl covered her head, hands

fluttering down as a candle flickered.

I was the ship that carried the grandmother.
If the family had stayed, mother's loins

too, would have been invaded. Daughter's negatives
crumpled, camera plate broken.

I broke the glass.

Forest-screams woke me, oil burning like a deer's
spoor, liquid welling into a pit. I imagined

breasts tossed from one man to another. I raised
my hands, chanted for a personal familiar.

I was taken from a music festival, distant spot
in the landscape, a single tree

scarred. A favorite blouse too tight around the arms,
bracelets digging ruts, dried blood. A crow

locked eyes with mine, hid my blemishes,
and after, took my bracelets and buried them.

I'm the names who didn't escape, marked
in the family tree a mother scripted—

child 1 child 2

Felting

I was told to let in the fibers,
and whatever dragon emerged from the Atlantic

crossing, fingers like stones, bleeding
clementines gone sour like something rotten

in the hold, as glass broken then ground,
as a baited trap for the hand,

I would bring.

       I was told to bring incipient
webs but felt was all I could manage,

the forgiving almost stiff hairs
escaping, thick braids unleashed

to batter the monster, reminder of the river
left behind (fish found easily),

I would bring.

       I was told to leach chartreuse
from lichen fingers where no vessel could harbor,

pilgrims seeking answers turned away,
instead nurses, maids, fishmongers, rabbis

and warriors, as dragonflies bottled then released,
as dandelions trailing fluff,

I would bring.

I was told, do not conceal the harbor,
do not scissor, do not bind or splint, do not wash

with soapy water, do not hook together
early, do not seascape,

and whatever tufts emerged
pulled gently,

I would bring.

I was told to scrunch cotton
with a clawed motion and whatever released

the trapped coursing, and let in
the paper-thin, the suckled

breast, the forgotten, the weighted,
the knife, the prey, the thieves, the angels

from another continent, the complainers,
the lost seagull with millinery straw in its beak,

I would bring.

Woman as an Aramaic Incantation Bowl

      curses of demons   curses of humans

    swallows of the wounded   I'm cursive scripted

smooth   rough   coiled

        find me hidden in a dusty corner

a threshold   a hillside   courtyard of the recently deceased   I'm dirt-

swallowed   beet-colored   beaten   lips on fire

    throat preserved these centuries

my clay absorbs grief   I hold

    a serpent eating its tail

        call him ordinary

    hidden in my bowels   but I'm rambling

        I can do the job

terracotta

(with or without eggshells encrusted)

I'm like an amulet   calm

on my knees   I bend over

stain the ground   chanting until

they bury me face down

    and the serpent within

        escapes

At the Market after Reading about the Alien Meteorite

I worry how much longer they'll stock peaches, almost
out of season with their shimmer hairs, or strawberries

already smushed and rotten. The produce manager arranges
varieties of apples and pears, when a woman gasps, finger

on the price tag for nectarines from a local farm. What choice
but to buy fruit while a fragment fireball threatens to crumb,

morsel, shiver us into dust? Called alien from a magma
ocean, special equipment required to witness

the glow. As I head to the meat counter, I consider my mother
at the Woolworths counter ordering liver and onions for us,

something my father and brother would never stand for.
Later, she'd say, *Can you feel the boost?* As if iron

swam through our blood-sweetness, cutting
the metallic taste. I envision the meteorite coming

from an iron-rich ocean. I wonder, how much chicken
needed for tacos. How happy should we be

when scientists talk about something called *true promise,*
where we can learn the galaxy's history,

because won't uncovering the truth reveal the underside
of fruit peel, tender strife of yellow, and explain

why my mother fortified us with liver? I'd rather stare
out windows to a streetlight where cars rev,

then speed away. On one shelf they've stocked
handmade crocheted hats and gloves. Maybe they've always

waited in a pile, not just for holidays. And despite the comet
at any moment closing in, crashing, I live for the Shangri-la

choosing of foods, planning four kinds of salsas,
and on another day Malabar curry, potatoes and cauliflower

with black mustard seed, and to accompany a salad, a honeyed chèvre
spread on walnut levain. Bodies without trajectory,

no interstellar activity. I reach into the refrigerator case
for sheep's milk yogurt from Sonoma, almost everything

checked off the list, when I overhear a customer asking for help—
can't find the fresh mozzarella, then mumbling,

No caprese tonight.

My Soul Blossom in Your Blood

I've been told, *Don't over prune,*
don't over water. I'm stumbling
on high heels, then trying
to eat breakfast, but it's a bowl
of blood. I take another breath,
then start over. This time
it's tangerines, heavy, thumping,
ticking like a camera shutter.
Did I hurl too many insults,
a learned tactic to dismember
the enemy's vocal chords? Mine
have broken. A man plays cello
at the border crossing, children
looking on who have hidden for years
among those who would keep them
after their parents were taken.

> After their parents were taken,
> among those who would keep them,
> looking on, hidden for years
> at the border crossing, children
> have broken. A man plays cello
> to the enemy's vocal chords. Mine
> a learned tactic to dismember—
> did I hurl too many insults,
> ticking like a camera shutter?
> It's tangerines, heavy, thumping,
> a starting over. This time
> blood. I take another breath
> to eat breakfast, but it's a bowl
> on high heels. Then try again.
> *Don't over water.* I'm stumbling.
> I've been told, *Don't over prune.*

I grow extra ovaries

while I sleep, dream of surplus bicycle wheels spinning,
mitochondria sworls, and how I'll need to compensate. I'll mark
myself with plastic slinkies, knock-offs of metal originals, push-
pin spirograph wheels on a board, then rotate. Am I to blame for
dysfunction, grapefruit-sized cyst occluding one ovary? Maybe
the Alaskan cruise, dolphins leaping ahead of the bow, too much
backstroke in the pool, upper deck? In one dream I call out,
High water from the ship's prow, then run inside past the bar
to pilfer pretzels. I hike backcountry at ports of call, past skunk
cabbage into Three Sisters wilderness. My friend says she doesn't
know how much time she has left, but don't we all feel that way
when called to the surgeon's table?

> early warning
> oh, Arteria Ovarica
> shoulders wrapped in crêpe

Pigment into a Wound

Perhaps the country wasn't ready, tormented
before the holy book

was written, shammash on hand
to bury the dead.

She'd had enough of the temple's halakha
dividing her from men, enough of border towns

invaded. Worried
she'd given her children

too much or not enough, or that fasting
wasn't enough

or what about the thin curtains
she'd hoped to replace.

She continued to apply deep red lipstick,
the only makeup she believed in

because belief, the exacting color
left by her ancestors

when revelation was in short supply,
moated her hunger.

Above a gorge, wild cypress
clung to a granite shelf,

and splintered cedar cried out,
no one a witness—

When the sky
missiled into her,

her eyes froze, reading
the words behind the text—

*This is the path
re-written in haste.*

Forceps of War

curled inside the safe-room // she remembers
floating in a sea of hospital-

white minerals with her mother

bullets
scream // grenade //

she texts *they're coming*

the last anyone hears //

// after

someone has to milk the cows

they took her // they left her body // they burned the safe-room
all these things are true

// now there is only rust

a girl's doll // porcelain arms
// pried off

rain resolves the pasture
calves are pulled out //

Savage

Not the Roman Empire but claws lashing
air, elephants flying to ground,

vulture finally meeting his match, cities pounded
until eyelids bandage, and a lone towhee

with an orange rump pierces her one-note
song before the approach.

They do not like crowds as humans do—
this is not the Colosseum, no *look-at-me* battle,

no outsiders. Sorrows gild in a garden.
No heaven or hell, animals climb an eternal

tightrope through atmosphere rungs
to a place without hierarchy, without angels,

and below, no demons.

A wolf's treasure not raided even if rampage
destroys flowers.

We are the trodders with our eyes that cling,
jaws that turn air. We who seduce

everything, hunger for the original garden,
an overturned version.

When the animals take over,
we then, passersby with no Godly notion—

just briefcase empty of paper
just savage.

Ask the Goats

Fable

The tree in the bird's mouth broke free,
then broke the bird down the middle like an egg.

Soothsayers who grew up near the tree can't pinpoint
a bronze moment when snow masqueraded as a field.

Children hurled streamers in a spring parade,
a town of hope that offered a horse's bridle

sewn by the star craftsman for a wedding couple.
No one noticed when the tree cracked.

The beak of the bird grew. *The exact same bird,*
one girl claimed, *grown from an egg last spring.*

The tree could only agonize about its own birth
when it spoke (and no human could hear)—

it said, *The devil has nothing to do with me.*
Such defensiveness! The tree couldn't be trusted

because only birds peddled their wares in these parts,
aside from the red fox, the mink, the hare, the bear.

Only thunder could cure the lichen branches,
only whispers could heal.

The Sacrificial Goat

i.

Finally a chill this morning at the Little Farm,
sweet smell of straw as I brush fur the wrong way
then close my arms around the bulbous chest cavity.

I draw the udders close, my throat dry
at the proximity of mother's milk.

                        Then withdraw
before one of the volunteers notices.

     I've come to ask the goats
about impermanence, caressing the horns—
smooth, rough, ridged.

                It's enough
to hear a *chirp* from the narrow face.

These goats will not be sacrificed.

ii.

     In one story of the ancient Israelites, atoning
for a year's worth of sins, they send a scapegoat, Azazel,
into the wilderness to carry those sins.

     Growing up, mother read a different story—
a boy sent with the family goat for slaughter.
Boy and goat caught in a snowstorm, dug under a haystack.
Goat ate the hay, boy drank her milk.

            Maa, she cried.
The boy heard her say, *We must accept heat, cold,
hunger, satisfaction, light and darkness.*

iii.

At the evening Yom Kippur service, the rabbi says
we no longer practice sacrifice.
                                        We rise
from folding chairs to stand—with discomfort—
we pay for our sins.

I never asked my father whether the tilt of a goat's head
was a way of reading mood.
            Or what the man atoned for yearly. Did he chasten
his tongue, how it curdled
                              during family yelling sessions?

Why he disappeared for days into a wilderness of city streets—
hardware store, city dump for car parts, unkosher
hamburgers, snacks in crisp paper wrappers.

iv.

            The goats at the Little Farm speak one line—
Maa. Maybe they're complaining to the rabbits,
caged so they won't run away, or the cow
inhaling carrots from a visitor's hand.

One goat's black stripe like a mohawk
suggests an outspoken temperament,
its eyes split in half like archers with a narrow gaze.

            No one needs to tell me
the ancient tribe of Benjamin were archers, warriors of Judea,
goat their symbol. People with split goat eyes.
Did they, like their namesake, inhabit fields with stone walls,
                              mayflies blinked away?

v.

At morning services the rabbi recounts the goat story.
She can't decide whether *Azazel* is the goat's name, wiry hair
curling into air like smoke, or the act of setting the goat free.

                        I have come here to stand
with my tribe, for Hebrew words that will somehow
absolve sins.
                Maybe the Aramaic, also cast onto holy pages,
        echo of ancient ritual, will do a better job.

                Then we say the names of the dead. I don't voice
my parents, instead whisper their soft and hard consonants to myself—
Thelma, Sol

                                into my scarf.

    For the holiday, mother withheld her Constant Comment tea
and father his Folgers coffee.

I have no sins to cast, no water to cross. I could confess
the ways in which I injure my husband, countering
the ways he injures me, but it wouldn't
                                be enough.

The Rabbi moves onto another story, another lesson,
leaving the goat.

vi.

        In the boy and goat story I grew up with,
after a week the storm ceases, then they walk the distance home.
Goat now part of the family.

And I ask, where is the goat, animal of my tribe?

The stakes are higher today and I can only wonder
what sacrifice is necessary when we're told
        in the words of the Torah,
                the future has already been cast.

I Hurry with Cornflowers

I hurry with cornflowers along a wide open road
to relatives hiding in a barn with goats,
youngest cousin whose image reflects mine,
who transposed Bach in her teens, notes exposed.

Relatives hide behind tanks with the goats,
never notes exposed, years already blackened,
yet they transpose Bach in their blackened veins,
the mare's hair tamed into a fast pony tail.

They're exposed walking twenty miles blackened
past abandoned car windows, street-shuttered,
long hair loosened from a pony tail, twirled
before arranging belongings in a clear vase.

Back home, dining room table street-shuttered,
youngest cousin whose image reflects mine
twirled, before arranging the future in a clear vase.
I fly through the sky with cornflowers held tight.

HOW TO QUILT ABSOLUTION

On Easter I Quote Ecclesiastes to My Husband

A time of breakfast where I remove one waffle from the iron,

crisp to retain syrup. A time to admit, no love story,

how we crawl into our bones. A time to tell Ecclesiastes

he neglected relationships, over-doing it on seasons. A time

for orange squeezing, swirl motion, cup placed

on a blue tablecloth. A time to cut chicken apple sausages

into pieces, *A little of this, a little of that,* said my father, who argued

with his conservative friend, didn't engrave too deeply,

didn't gift-wrap a sentence, *mishpatim* a skill not blood-based.

A time to tell my husband, I'm worried about Passover after Jews

in Israel couldn't fold dough over filling on Purim, missiles

raining in the north. A time where my people, enslaved, left Egypt,

depended on Moses' correspondence with God. A time to learn

how apples came via the Silk Road to the Holy Land. A time to repair

my covenant with God, once broken playing hangman

with Betsy Zeff in Hebrew class, then running

to the convenience store for gum. A time to unpoison the future.

A time when my husband in a little robe clasped hands, altar boy

preparing to forget the rules. A time to say out loud,

the holy book is continually rewritten and we can interpret. A time

when waffles cannot support berries, fried egg running wild.

When my husband on our wedding anniversary

leans across the table at the hole-in-the-wall restaurant
and says, *The tamale's all herbs* and puts his forks down,

I say, *Mine's plump*, legions of pork falling away
from crumbly masa. The owner approaches,

finger on lips, *Beware of the chili*, as if she could provide
the marriage safe passage. She sees beyond

multi-color flags and laminated wood tables
to our kiss. Walking home, our steps,

once an embrace, now a precipice.
I imagine Romeo and Juliet in Verona,

near the market, off a side street crammed with tourists,
where one-at-a-time, someone stands on the balcony

and yells down to a beloved or a friend pretending
to be a beloved. Because aren't we all Juliet?

Her story, seeking the friar, combining all the seasons
into her clouded heart—what tips would she dispense right now—

Go to the sea, check an easy-to-read inspiration pamphlet,
worship God not magic—or are her secrets lost?

Now, I dress for all eventualities, could survive in the woods,
choose berries for ink, because didn't my people

survive off manna in the desert forty years? The truth is
I haven't learned to harvest acorns, yet I climb the hills

where natives once lived, find a grinding stone to reveal
the seed inside the fruit, where flour leached in a stream

removes bitterness, where a sheltered camp means
the long reaching branches of an oak.

Cat as Muse

We are not idealized wild things
    —Joan Didion, *Magical Thinking*

The cat swipes her paw on the tv screen when mice appear,
    pokes her head behind the monitor, growls as noses

dart and little bodies dig a dirt mound. She's figured out
    how to peel back a scent of dirt, runs on a fur-scattered

trail into darkness. After my mother died, I connected
    stars with hand-drawn lines like fairy lights.

And standing in the night garden, I wondered
    what's unknowable beyond science, synapses firing.

Hunting for shadows of planets, Venus wooed Jupiter,
    distance so close. Every time the cat gallops over, rises

on hind legs like a Meerkat, jumps on the tv table,
    she swats long tails. When the mouse tunnels through,

she follows. Joan Didion's husband died one evening
    at the dining room table. She thought she might

summon her husband back to life. In my own grief,
    I blurred past and present, losing the self I knew.

Couldn't bring my mother back, though tried in ghost
    conversations on daily walks. Perhaps I ran away.

Today, I release my child brain, move close to the tv,
    extend my tongue and lick the writhing mouse belly,

kangaroo hind legs, pointed witches with noses so delicate,
    diaphanous ears like window panes, where I find

my mother, find what's been smuggled out of this world,
    past tears in the corners of the sky.

Self-Portrait as a Tea Shop

Is it better to be the woman at the counter who rubs cups,
notched-neck priestess? Or better to be a Zhejiang picker

who's never seen my insides yet fills the jars? I can't change
the harvest season, leaves dictating supply. A man arrives,

sits stands sits, then another chair, facing east. I encourage
workers to be mellow because that's the vibe we sell.

Can't stop a daughter's fingers thrumming, when her father
pushes my front door—*swoosh*—mushing the quiet

wood walls, wood floors, wood tables—*Your mother's
waiting*, he says. Can't stop today's eclipse, shadows

pressing floor-to-ceiling windows. Is it better
to be glass barring the rage of day? Better to darken

rage like River Puerh's earth and silk, a fermented
burgundy? I can't stop the betrayal of poppyseeds escaping

a cookie, rolling off the table, can't help but grumble—
slow down—then laugh when a woman reaches

for the teapot, knocking it down. Can't stop a man typing,
clumps of hair all that's left covered by a hoodie—

would offer Clouds and Mist, Yunwu tea tips curled
into spirals, buttery smooth. I can't stop the dying.

Is it better to be liquid, adhere to a surface
unchangeable? Better to be orange-yellow buckwheat's

criminal nuttiness, or bright green sencha tearing its mouth
from the glass? Better to be bread of the earth in a teapot?

Better to infuse the tongue with bitterness?

How to Quilt Absolution

Morning after surgery, you cut three-point leaves,
six-point stars, more sawtooth lines
than cloth deserves.

        Years ago, a teacher demonstrated
the basic running stitch then backstitched
her students, no mention

of how other skills like map reading,
creating a new recipe, writing characters
into short fiction would sharpen the eye.

Images of ships or castles wouldn't
prepare fabric or thread a machine,
yet each stitch individually

would catch all layers within the quilt.
She ran through patterns—Broken Plaid,
Hanging Diamond, True Lover's Knot.

You chose Twisted Rope.

        Today, you walk only ten minutes.
The abdomen will take months to repair incisions,
removal of the mass.

You would rather know how to shape trapunto trees,
piece together a cloth of absolution
but the quilt doesn't follow anyone else's story,

cushioned against attack, padded against chill.
You remember the teacher spoke of an Egyptian
Pharaoh and the quilted cloak he wore

so followers would marvel. Leaving
that final class, one woman laughed,
I should be banished from quilting altogether.

You reminded her to sew
with thread made of cotton,
not too taut so it doesn't shrink in the wash.

Dear Ovary, My Music Seed

I brewed you from a delicious wrath of sheet music, from
reluctant vocal chords. Paid no mind to the violinist's arm close
to my oboe, both of us addicted to melody, while cello and bass
kept time. I had no song of my own, instead pieced together
Bach's counterpoint. I took no responsibility for your gut-ripe
casing, your taut-strung closing. Like an invisible architect who
cut a flip book. You heard, *Largo ma non tanto*. Slowly. Now,
I sing without an instrument, soloist without a music room,
circled by gowns in an operating theater. The Italian doctor's
tools suck liquid, pincers remove fibers.

>   oh, this lopsided body
>   a tiny round music book
>
>   dollhouse wallpaper
>
>   I sing, *oh come loose*
>   *into the ether*

Motel Room Without a Night Light

I open doors in the middle of the night,
like a game show, three knobs where I have to choose.

What can I do except stub my toe? My husband and I
have arrived to follow birds, hike coastal trails,

eat local bread encrusted with sesame seeds—not to escape
our friend, taken to the ICU, and his wife's

recaps of each new protocol. A few years ago,
he helped curate the *Summer of Love* exhibit.

We followed him through galleries—heard about
Better Living Through Chemistry, a poster

on psychedelics. Heard how he met Ben,
whose visual-acid footage covered the audience,

the walls, the band on stage at Winterland. As we filed
through the exhibit, color and image stained

our skin. We heard about the *March to End
the Vietnam War* poster, when my father

in the VW Squareback drove our friend to Kezar stadium,
up and down San Francisco hills, along with his mother

because he wasn't old enough. Heard about the poster
Help, the Oracle Needs You Today, the Haight Ashbury

underground paper. And this week, he is installed
in a new cancer center, harboring tumors so plentiful

there's no middle back left. Today, on our hike
in Point Reyes, down to the sea, we didn't know he received

his first chemo drip. Told by nurses
he could hallucinate, he found an aura in the room,

flashes of color. Found Oneness because he knows
how to love. And here I am, in the middle of the night,

trying to find my way, standing still for a minute.
There's a full moon coming through the skylight.

Woman under the Bridge

Today no sign of her pushing a loaded cart,
instead squawking about a bum leg
as I pass the bridge, no sign
of flowing gown and tossed hair.

I remember one student on probation
from prison, his admission, living under
a bridge and at ten years old, creeping into
a video store, selling to the underbelly.

I walk as if I could keep the growing things
awake and clasp their power into
my life—monkey puzzle trees lining the path,
gnarls changing sun-patterns.

I can't help this woman who churls her fist
at fast walkers in zipped-up sweatsuits,
anyone who comes close, or a slow
moving bike with a boom-box. Her eyes

pour fine dust, not tears. Leaves twine
into her hair like a dryad-mix-tape.
On my walk back she's there, feet
dangling over the creek near a young stand

of redwoods. Do I hear a prayer or
am I examining my conscience?
What vow will stop birds flying into glass
or snails called invasive from scoring

their own song—all the vows will not stop
the narrative. This is not an elegy for the woman
who lost everything—she sewed tight
that decree before the time of Moses.

In my garden, I refill the bird bath.
It's already autumn in my mouth.

THE ART OF PERSUASION

Ars Poetica as Crochet

You are crocheting fog
        in the backyard so buttery
roses mother grows
        will turn yellow-red,
an in-between like the mezzo-
        soprano she blasts
on the radio. In fact you are crocheting
        your life to fill in
empty spaces—it's not enough
        she taught you to read—
no yarn will pull her in
        from full time work.
You wait on father to return
        from nights counseling,
crocheting a briefcase
        containing notes for
how to love you.
        You crochet memories
of Christmas when you're Jewish,
        perfectly shaped triangle
with cats underneath. Still,
        the picture of yourself
doesn't fit. Then you crochet
        the bay, mountain on the far side,
and an invisible train, horn
        blaring, metal wheels
metal track, fifteen minutes by the clock
        solid steady
repairing your parent's absence.
        At night the doorknob turns,
ghost of family who escaped Poland
        in 1920 entering your room
asking to be crocheted
        in Yiddish, language

you have no yarn for
        but somehow in gestures
a place is filled in,
        every stitch.

The Art of Persuasion

i.

Toothbrush in little hands half-filled with paste,
back and forth
      as the girl's mother scolds, *Esther, you know better,*
remember to share.

Campground bathroom mirror reflects mother and daughter,
eyes sideways, long auburn hair—
I do not ask about the ends waving like grasses
close to the river.

I do not ask, *Campground Esther, what spell have you cast this time?*

As a girl, I fell in love with Bible Esther,
where the curve of her cheek stood against injustice,
where she saved Persian Jews from a pogrom.

Will Campground Esther escape punishment
      like her namesake?

ii.

I'm twelve years old at the temple Purim bazaar,
hamantaschen cookies, dough folds revealing
poppyseed, prune, or apricot filling,
like stained glass,
      The cookie type, not as good, my mother says,
preferring the sweetless dough made in our kitchen.

She buys me a L'Chai pendant,
      says it means *Life*.

My brother and I run the hallway.
Fingering the pendant, I realize I'm old enough
for life,
        which is adulthood, isn't it?

    iii.

In the campground bathroom, tall pointed windows
let in the redwoods,

        when bird calls begin—
the dripping bird, we named it, like a faucet,
and another, high-pitched echo of the marbled murrelet,
belonging to the ocean but married old growth,
upper stories nest-laden.

I'm waiting for the one sink with warm water,
to open pores, saturate with cleanser.

        Wait
for the foam of conversation to simmer.

    iv.

What Esther and her mother don't know—
in my campsite I'm tangled in blame
for a nephew's relationship fail.

Such nonsense.

        My husband: *your communication style is different.*

(What he believes: *why does she have to be the bird
        who doesn't belong?*)

But it's more than that. I imagine others unmasked
for their plots to murder, like Bible Esther's cunning villain.
A story where God is not mentioned.

I don't want to hide my identity,
        say, *I'm Jewish, a scapegoat.*

I will not be made invisible.

        v.

Esther places her toothbrush on the sink ledge,
hand resting on the immalleable surface.

        You're right, Mama. I'll apologize to her.

Her face cinematic, shifts from toil to dreams.
        She is the froth of hot chocolate
when people emerge from tents like bears from the lair.

There's something fixed about the scene,
mother's instructions,
        yet does anyone know
                how a girl will respond?

Maybe she'll return to her campsite, share her bike
with her cousin.

        She will learn in reflection,
lead us through diaspora.

The Quarrel

Break potted African violets, plump and satisfied
on the dining room table.
                              Mother fades
                    into a thicket of fog.

          Break dishes and glassware.

Father's underarms a damp crescent. Wipes
his forehead with a large handkerchief.

Studies Freud and Jung, wise men. Breaks
the door.

I wonder how any of us normalites
could become a prophet

when we break
                    pencils,

betray God in our ritual arguments.

My brother's no tightrope artist, rises
to the ceiling with a flaming tongue.

He is the ghost of family
from the past—

                    Poland in the days of empire.

Then he's broken (bruises only later
discovered) skull peeking

                              out of his forehead
as if he can grow faster.

Jews don't have a third eye,
but witnessing the bruises is our job.

Hourglass

The dream of trapped figures repeats. This time they speak of breakfast, one woman's hat resembles a fried egg, another woman's hair dyed purple like her German teacher who served salami the final day of class. A woman wearing a striped apron crosses her arms—she will not prepare the meal. The egg drips and covers legs until the lower halves of their bodies disappear. When I awaken I know they have no provisions for survival, but the logic ends there.

On your shelf of journals you'll find lists, descriptions of problems, complaints, story fragments, as well as dreams. Burn these hardcover books so no one can bridge the ice cave to town. Throw away the ladder. Crosshatch problem-solving lists. Tear A & B columns in half. Remove pith from an orange segment.

The dream of trapped figures repeats. This time a townscape with figures, women flapping their arms in an ice cave near a pueblo. How ice and heat meet makes no sense, yet *Ooos* of crystal chill until fingers fall off. Bare feet accidentally crunch the digits. The paper-thin dresses turn to water as they discuss how to sew another layer. Where would they find material? Soft stucco shapes fade into clouds like they've birthed mountains.

Nine Months Post-October 7

Months ago the obgyn cauterized   to repair a surgical error
After   I sat in dusk   under the magnolia   swallowtail
washing iridescent

And now
     it's enough   to sit down to new fabric   washed and ironed
sewing machine fitted   slender thread   seaming a natural
slant to the skirt   running along wide hips

Wind scrapes the window   when I lament women in another country
taken hostage nine months ago   chained to an olive tree
branches   a string-tied bouquet
                         and further   to houses where men
         command

             I want   to picture instead   new trees
planted on a hillside   salt clustering the edge   dissolving
         and the sea beyond
                             reflective

And each granule of my body says
                         Bring home the young women   pregnant

Today my husband asks
                         Did the doctor appointment go well
I groan
         Right you've never seen an obgyn
         where gestation   is a threat
                         where swallowtail wings   batter the air
July already gone to seed

Our Life Is the Life of Bread

Decades ago in Jerusalem, a woman
      blew herself up at a house of bread,
sesame seeds and poppyseeds the fallen.
      Her longing, to own time

that Shabbat, human organs
      cut open by nails, loaves removed
from the oven in bits   weary   dry
      leaping onto the street.

I envision what my father would say
      about bread and how it requires
cured meats   salt   sweet   fat
      and how coleslaw and smoked

whitefish sides paired with corned beef
      lain flat on a bed of rye,
wiping his face clean. But he is not here
      to witness   boiled   baked   risen—

oven drama, crowds chanting
      as they set off smoke bombs outside
a Holocaust memorial. Others night-scrawl
      red markings on a politician's door,

storm campuses like yeast rising.

People Speak Yiddish in Bars All over Berlin

There's a break in the skirt panel of a woman who elbows
an oak table, beer on her shoes in the Berlin bar.

She says, *Verklempt*, when words stop then continue. Only
I don't speak Yiddish so would miss the *mishpatim*,

argument between two men settled with compromise.
I wonder about my great-grandfather who thrust

hands into a herring barrel to buy enough for Shabbat,
and my grandparents who suitcased from Poland,

ship's hull assaulted with water until the water
spoke Yiddish, but swallowed the tail of a fish

to cloud memory. On arrival, their New York
apartment spoke what sounded like German

but was not German—each sentence, yes,
each one, with a verb in the second place.

Today, people speak Yiddish all over Berlin, not written
in books of a lost civilization, but captured

in photos taken days before the glass broke—
some words stutter in stiff conversation,

meaning rapid hoof beats, some form the same arc
my grandmother pointed to in the sky the morning

they boarded the ship, remaining moon
lit by a new sun. Her father said, stroking his beard,

*Already compromise is written
into the curve of the sea's open throat.*

The Red Stairway

Where my family didn't subscribe
        to herbs or potions, only rational theory,
case studies at best, though the fridge
        stocked a whipped butter tub, fewer calories
but the same only fooling, so you see,
        suspension of disbelief plays into this story.

Where father drove past cypress trees
        on the coast road as we lurched, windows
rolled down to witness rock tumbling to waves,
        then over and under the historic bridge,
decorous arch where summer lived, where we tented,
        pumped the stove, soaked our toes.

Where the opaque milk-kosher dishes
        for B.B. and Beckie were first cleansed
of soil. We accepted Silly Putty purchased
        at Discount Mart. I did not consider, as B.B.
leafed through the Jewish newspaper,
        how he'd left and lost Russia.

Where my mother's middle expanded
        and gilded my brother. She forested
nasturtiums in the side yard while he
        skipped into the wild, later carrying him
when a lung collapsed, hands trembling—
        who trembled, she or him.

Where my refugee grandmother knitted
        a lace prayer. She and her mother climbed
a painted red stairway, climbed to a new land
        where in a park they shadowed robins,
chimed, *Old world bird* to their narrow beaks,
        their dark lashes.

In the Middle

i.

Ghosts dreamed the space between my parents.
I read the reflection in their longing (though I didn't know
the ache.) Grown love to suit my own purpose,
wind outside a river house singing to reeds and catkins,
foghorn where soffits unseen—could they reveal
creatures encased in silt robes? Older child,
I should have known, stories of marriage sodden
between elements.

ii.

Now I'm left to parse a marriage, our voices
soil sifted in excavation. Maybe one day
small household idols mentioned in the Bible as lost
will be discovered behind a shelf, intact. *Don't worry,*
says Jacob, who placates others, strategies of a businessman
more than a warrior, fooling other tribes
to save his own.

iii.

On Passover, we are Jews escaping slavery in Egypt,
the host saying, *Answer questions where
there are no answers*, to acknowledge the mess
between nations. Most want peace, as if
they've stashed away electric memories and only now
reveal them, as if peace ever materialized. One man says
he was born the year Israel was made a state
and would like that spirit to return.

We sing, *Let My People Go*

iv.

We recite plagues in unison, dip fingers in wine,
lay drops out one-by-one on our plate. *Dam - blood.*
Told to feel sorry for killing of the firstborn. We've suffered
and should help others who suffer. Then my stomach
aches. I trickle blood on the plate
of my parents' marriage and my own.

v.

I'm no longer in the middle about anything, argue
in-between courses, when I lean forward
to grab a bowl of charoset, apples and nuts
mortared with wine—don't notice when the candles
catch my hair—and the burning, and the soot.
No, we won't squirrel around politics.
Finally, others are laughing and it doesn't matter
over what.
We sing.
      We sing.

Notes

Many of my poems were inspired by artwork presented in my ekphrastic writers group.

Epigraph
Denise Levertov, "Making Peace" from *Breathing the Water*, New Directions Publishing Corporation, 1987.

[26] "Half the green donkey left Russia" is inspired by Marc Chagall's *L'âne Vert* (The Green Donkey) (Russia), 1911.

[35] "Woman Posing as Bell Pepper" is inspired by the photograph *Bell Pepper No. 30* by Edward Weston (USA), 1930.

[39] "Anti-Love Poem" is in conversation with Grace Paley's "Anti-Love Poem." Also inspired by Michaela Yearwood-Dan's artwork *The only way is up* (England), 2021.

[43] "Roundup of Children from the Ghetto" is inspired by Max Ernst's *33 Little Girls Chasing Butterflies* (Germany), 1958. Ernst did not have the experience of the speaker in the poem, though he was in Camp des Milles, a French internment camp, considered to be an enemy alien. Two years later he escaped to the United States with the help of Peggy Guggenheim.

[46] "Letter to the Angels, Poland, 1919" refers to Psalms 74:14—Leviathan appears as a multi-headed sea serpent; Isaiah 27:1—Leviathan slain by God; Job 41—Job is eaten by the creature. The resource is *Letters to Mary 1911–1919: Chronicling the Weinreb Family's Life in Europe, Pre-immigration and During World War I*, prepared by Ellen Weinreb, 2025. My cousin Marion Kaselle stored these letters for some time, not knowing what they were. Cousin Ellen Weinreb took them, had the Yiddish, Polish, and German languages translated, then organized the project. She is having them archived with the YIVO Institute for Jewish Research in New York. They are letters mainly from my great-grandfather Avrum Mordecai (Markus) to his children, though others including my grandmother have a part. Two of the children immigrated prior to 1920; the rest journeyed in 1920. Those left behind perished in the Holocaust.

[52] "I follow my mother through the gallery" refers to the exhibit *Mary Cassatt at Work*, at the Legion of Honor museum, San

Francisco, 2024. The beginning of the poem is inspired by Julie Mehretu's artwork *Among the Multitude XIII* (Ethiopia / USA), 2021.

[59] "A Blind Day Where Our Porch is Soaked" is in conversation with Wendell Berry's "Peace of Wild Things."

[60] "Diaspora" is inspired by Ana Mendieta's *Untitled: Silueta Series, Mexico* (Cuba), 1976, a photograph of a crack in the ground that she shaped into a woman, and blood thrown in. In the Silueta Series she merged the female figure with the earth, reminiscent of ancient goddess forms. The locations were outside Havana where indigenous people once lived. Her political life and trauma, as well as her suspicious death, also inspired me to write about my own people's trauma, in a persona poem.

[64] "Woman as an Aramaic Incantation Bowl" refers to incantation bowls from the sixth through eighth centuries, viewed as a form of protective magic. They were inscribed in Jewish Aramaic. The bowls refer to themselves as "amulets." The Talmud discusses the use of amulets and magic to drive away demons. The bowls were used by ordinary people whereas the scribes originated from a range of social, educational, and religious backgrounds. Scholars' understanding of these bowls is a watershed in studying Jewish magic and amulets.

[65] "At the Market after Reading about the Alien Meteorite" responds to a news article in *Nature* magazine by Alexandra Witza: "An 'alien meteorite' probably didn't slam into earth—how will we know if one does?" September 6, 2023.

[67] "My Soul Blossom in Your Blood" is inspired by the photo of Mistislav Rostropovitsch playing cello at Checkpoint Charlie, November 11, 1989, when the Berlin Wall came down, taken by Sgt L. Emmett Lewis Jr. (USA).

[69] "Pigment into a Wound" is inspired by Muriel Rukeyser's "Poem (I lived in the first century of world wars)." The end refers to the midrash idea of how the holy book is continually rewritten and this is "the path."

[72] "Savage" is inspired Franz Rosel von Rosenhof's artwork *After the Fall of Man* (Germany), 1690.

[77] "The Sacrificial Goat" refers to the Isaac Bashevis Singer story "Zlateh the Goat." The poem is also inspired by Marc Chagall's *La*

Veste Rouge (Russia), 1961, in considering the transformation of goat and boy and how they survive, and the transformations possible on the Jewish New Year. Thanks to the goats at Little Farm, Tilden Regional Park, Berkeley, California.

[80] "I Hurry with Cornflowers" is inspired by Tetyana Yablonska's *Seeds* (Ukraine), 1969. Also responds to a news article in the BBC News, Poland: "Ukraine Conflict: Refugees rush to borders to flee Russia's war," Mark Lowen, February 25, 2022.

[85] "When my husband on our wedding anniversary" is inspired by *A Theory of Doors* by Kristen Holt-Browning. I had to consider what kind of theories Juliet would come up with for survival in order to invent my own version.

[86] "Cat as Muse" is inspired by Max Ernst's *Some Animals are Illiterate* (Germany), 1973. While animals may be illiterate, they have other powers, including imagination.

[87] "Self-Portrait as a Tea Shop" is in conversation with Agi Mishol's "Better" (translated by Joanna Chen) and Saba Kermati's "Self-Portrait as a Bowl of Persimmons."

[91] "Motel Room Without a Night Light" refers to the *Summer of Love Experience* exhibit at the DeYoung Museum, San Francisco, 2017.

[96] "Ars Poetica as Crochet" is inspired by Hadara Bar-Nadav's "Family of Strangers," in particular her phrase "Ghosts multiply, spreading while I sleep."

[98] "The Art of Persuasion" refers to Esther as she is described in the Aprocrypha, parts removed from the Bible. "Do not imagine, Esther, that of all the Jews in the kingdom you alone will be safe" (Mardochaeus).

[101] "The Quarrel" is inspired by Marc Chagall's *The Quarrel* (Russia), 1914.

[102] "Hourglass" is inspired by Elisabeth Vellacott's *Townscape with Figures (I)* (England), 1905–2002. Her work is delicate yet reveals intense scenes—in some, a crowd at the cliffs; in another, the sighting of Lazarus; and in this piece, women inside a cave, yet near enough to a town. I had to consider the reason for their hideaway.

[103] "Nine Months Post-October 7" is inspired by Ben Shahn's *Barbed Wire Paradise* (Lithuania / USA), 1959. I considered the spaces women find themselves in during political conflict. Shahn himself was a social activist, an orthodox Jewish émigré.

[104] "Our Life Is the Life of Bread" is inspired by Agi Mishel's *Shaheeda*, which recounts the story of a female who blew herself up at an Israeli market bakery. Also inspired by Sharon Hass's "Our Life is the Life of Beasts."

[105] "People Speak Yiddish in Bars All over Berlin" responds to a news article in the *Forward*: "You can now hear people speaking Yiddish in bars all over Berlin," by Rosamond van Wingerden, February 18, 2024.

A San Francisco Bay Area native, born and raised, Laurel's writing is sculpted by the coastal landscape, foghorns, and trains, but also by the stories of her ancestors. Her work has been recognized widely. Her book, *Flowers on a Train* (Sheila-Na-Gig Editions, 2025), was finalist for the Cider Press Book Award and Honorable Mention for the Small Harbor Publishing Laureate Prize. She is a finalist for *The Ekphrastic Review* contests, has received Honorable Mention for the Ruben Rose Memorial Poetry Competition, Honorable Mention from OPA (Oregon Poetry Association), and holds Pushcart Prize and Best-of-the-Net nominations. She has been interviewed by *The Ekphrastic Review* and *Flapper Press*. Her poems appear in *Pirene's Fountain, Lily Poetry Review, Taos Journal of Poetry, Mom Egg Review,* and elsewhere. Her work has also been anthologized in *Women in a Golden State* (Gunpowder Press, 2025), *The Nature of Our Times* (Paloma Press, 2025), among others. Laurel is active with the Bay Area Women's Poetry Salon and is a reader for *Common Ground Review*. She founded and leads Ekphrastic Writers, a group dedicated to writing and community. Laurel holds an MFA in Fiction from Mills College. She is a former temp worker, children's book buyer, and community college English instructor. She invented a secret language with her brother. Learn more at laurelbenjamin.com

SHANTI ARTS

NATURE · ART · SPIRIT

Please visit us online
to browse our entire book catalog,
including poetry collections and
non-fiction books on nature, healing,
art, and more.

Also take a look at our highly
regarded art and literary journal,
Still Point Arts Quarterly, a feast for
the eyes and the imagination—
available to download for free.

www.shantiarts.com